TUBURU
LIVING THE LEGEND

GESIERE BRISIBE-DORGU

authorHOUSE®

AuthorHouse™
1663 Liberty Drive
Bloomington, IN 47403
www.authorhouse.com
Phone: 1 (800) 839-8640

Published by AuthorHouse 06/28/2019

ISBN: 978-1-5462-3508-8 (sc)
ISBN: 978-1-5462-3506-4 (hc)
ISBN: 978-1-5462-3507-1 (e)

Library of Congress Control Number: 2018903682

Print information available on the last page.

DEDICATION

This book is dedicated to all the known and unknown heroes of Izon-ebe. May your indomitable spirits continue to strengthen all who strive to make a difference in the Niger Delta and the world.

Contents

ACKNOWLEDGMENTS

I owe the completion of this book to the many persons who encouraged and gave me information about the great Tuburu. I am especially grateful to the following:

The late chaplain of the Rivers State University of Science and Technology Catholic Chaplaincy Rev. Fr. Udiakabong E.Umoren, who started me off by insisting that I read some biographies before commencing the research. In addition to giving me a couple of biographical books, he also suggested an outline and counseled that I endeavor to 'situate things in context' at all times.

Dr. Tipa Tom Tuburu, who patiently answered questions contained in a long questionnaire I sent to him and kept giving me updates over a period of ten years; the time it took me to complete my research.

Late Chief Victor Alale also provided invaluable information and patiently read through the manuscript, making useful corrections and observations.

Mr. Napolean Alale, who continues to be a worthy ally was the rock upon which my research was founded. He it was, who took all the pictures of Tuburu's fighting tools used in this book. He also provided regular updates and tidbits about Tuburu's awesome powers.

Many thanks to late Ebomo John Dorgu for his insight and contributions. I am also grateful to Mr. Wenepre Nanade and late Chief Clifford Nekade for their contibutions. I owe a debt of gratitude to the erudite Professor Joe Ebiware for his eagle-eyed proofreading. Mbana-O!

Thanks a million, to late Chief Naitri Ezonbodo, alias Nainai Power, for the enthusiasm and support he showed at the beginning of the project. The late Coleman Tuburu, alias mandolley, also deserves thanks for the encouragement he gave me. Thanks also to Mrs. Igbokwe Chioma for typing the manuscript.

INTRODUCTION

The name TUBURU is a familiar one to most Izon (Ijaw) speaking people not necessarily as the name of an individual but as a description of some Ijaw clans living along the Nun River. However, the TUBURU referred to in this book is the name of a man, perhaps the greatest warrior the *Tarakiri* clan of the Niger Delta has ever known. This colorful personality was born in **Agbere** in present day Bayelsa State, Nigeria, at an unknown date and died in 1895. I began hearing stories about his exploits several decades ago and decided to do a little research on him to assuage my curiosity and possibly, to unravel the TRUE TUBURU.

Information gathering began in earnest, in 1994. Questionnaire, oral history, literature review and colonial records formed the methodology. The main data was supplied by direct descendants of Tuburu. Dr. Tipa Tom Tuburu, a grandson of Tuburu; late Chief Victor Alale, a great grandson of Tuburu; Mr. Napoleon Alale, another great grandson of Tuburu and many others from the community, who had heard about Tuburu from their parents and grandparents. It is worthy of note that the oral accounts have remained fairly consistent in spite of the passage of time.

Tuburu was, from all accounts, a simple, yet complex man. He lived according to the laws of nature, as understood by ancient Izons. Incredible powers were and are usually bestowed on those who seek to understand the truth in their environment and Tuburu took full advantage of this and was truly blessed. Life in his day was full and exciting as it is today and in some cases even more so. The people lived in harmony with nature and it rewarded them with secrets that protected them from fearsome enemies of the natural, supernatural, inanimate and animate kinds.

The traditional beliefs of the people were based as usual, on their understanding and perception of what the environment held for them. Persons of a different hue like the early European traders and explorers were viewed with suspicion, fear and grave concern. Marvel, dear readers at how these European 'intruders' were attacked and battled valiantly by the so-called barbarians, using whatever weapons they had at their disposal be it spear, arrow, machete or Dane gun. Remember that warfare was at its primitive best at the time in question. Fighters relied solely on what they could invent to match their sphere of operation which was in many cases limited to their immediate locality and environs. Their primary concern was fending off intruders and attackers. One can imagine then the enormous challenge the sudden appearance of Caucasian traders presented.

Tuburu's life was a fantastic celebration of romance, courage, raw strength and unconditional patriotism. A person of his pedigree, charisma, power and importance could not avoid envy, intrigue, blackmail, admiration and hatred, in any age and so it was with him. Why was it so? Could it be attributed to just human nature or was it the result of a deeper 'something?' Please feel free to draw your own conclusions after you have read the entire book.

There is much to learn about the riverine Izon people of the Nigerian Niger Delta and their neighbors. They are a fascinating group and this book will give you a glimpse into their world.

A GLIMPSE

Bare-chested and with determined long strides, he moved towards the townsquare. Little children took one look at his hairy body and burst into tears, burying their heads inside their mothers' petticoats. Men discreetly walked backwards and slipped into their mud thatch-roofed houses. The women however cheered, waving scarves or wrappers intoning;

"Olotu! Ongulobiagulobia, Ogbajeneke! Owei! Owei ke owei! Miena-adia-ey!"

All the dogs in the town would come out, wag their tails vigorously and sit quietly. The line-up of these dogs alone was in itself, a spectacle to behold.

By the time he got to the dusty square, the place was deserted except for the *Bebeare-owei*.

"Where is everyone? Where are those who want to challenge me?" the now sweaty champion asked, looking around.

"*Apoo* Odudu! Who dares wrestle with you when you are like this? Sweat pouring from your body like water, the hairs on your chest, hands and legs glistering and dark! Even your height has increased, making you equal to a twenty-year old palm tree! And look! Your body is vibrating like a canoe being beaten by waves! Who indeed can stand before you Odudu?" asked the *Bebeare-owei*.

"Yes! Who indeed can hold on to the slippery electric fish?" Both men turned in the direction of the voice and there, with a faint smile on his face was the *Orukare-owei* in person. He was highly respected by all because of his dual role as chief priest and medicine man.

"*Kare-owei*, I am surprised to see you here, surely…"

"My son Tuburu listen," the *Orukare-owei* interrupted.

"It is an irresponsible father who folds his hands and watch when strangers bust into his house. I know who you are. Try not to listen to fools when they boast. Odudu! Go home. We shall arrange a proper wrestling contest to coincide with *Owu-oge*."

"*Kare-owei* you have spoken. You are my mentor and father of all, I cannot disobey you. I will go home." Tuburu responded, leaving the arena.

He was just seventeen years old, when the above incident took place. Tuburu was muscular and imposing. No young man in his age group was as big as him and his size was backed by raw strength, as attested to by close friends and family. According to Bogha his elder brother,

"I went to cut firewood with Tuburu one day. When we got to the forest, I told him to concentrate on the northern section while I went west. I figured that we needed at least four hours of work to fill the big boat we used that day. But just one hour later, he called and said it was time to go home. I was amazed to discover that he had single-handedly cut enough wood to fill the boat!"

Others also spoke of Tuburu's abilities in like manner.

"He can kill animals with his bare hands! No! Not only small ones but the big cats- leopards, tigers and lions. The only animals he killed with spear were elephants and hippopotamus."

Tuburu's brothers, Asima and Abinaye were very proud of him. It was from them many in the community learnt that a big calamity was averted.

"The three of us were coming back from Abueto market when we saw a group of armed men. Their canoe was tied to a small tree near *Toru-abobou* sandbank. Not knowing who they were, we cautiously anchored our canoe a short distance from the group, without being seen. Tuburu volunteered to spy on them. He went right into the bush and returned after a short while to inform us that the conversations that transpired among the armed men, involved a planned attack on Agbere. In fact, three additional boats were being awaited. When we suggested that the community be informed immediately Tuburu refused.

"No! I will deal with them. I want you to distract them from the river while I go on land and surprise them."

This gallant young man eliminated ten of the men, while two were allowed to escape.

Tuburu was known as a man of few words. He did not like to be drawn into unnecessary arguments.

"I see no reason to involve myself in such talk. Nothing can be gained. It is a waste of time," he would say.

He had a special relationship with the *Orukare-owei*. The friendship between them was so strong that he spent several hours with him every day. Many began to speculate whether Tuburu was in fact a reincarnation of the *Orukare-owei*'s father. The man was reputed to be the strongest man in the entire clan when he was alive. Belief in reincarnation was as natural to the people as night and day. Indeed, it was taken for granted. Another firmly held belief was the continuous link between the ancestors and the living. There was no break in communication as loved ones always 'heard' from the dead either through dreams, seers or the *Orukare-owei*. Tuburu, like most warriors was never afraid of death.

"Death?" he would question.

"There is no death. We mingle with the ancestors every day. They guide and show us things so where is the so-called death?" he would ask, smiling.

THE IZONS (Ijaws)

HISTORY AND GEOGRAPHY

Residing along the Eastern to the Western shores of Nigeria, the Ijaws are undeniably one of the oldest inhabitants of the Niger Delta. They are a seafaring people and have always lived predominantly along the Coast. The people have had a checkered history both in ancient and modern times. One indisputable fact about the Ijaws is that they were and still are a peace loving and hospitable people. They generally avoid situations that would bring conflict while not shying away from defending themselves if attacked. This informed their choice of settlements along the banks of various rivers, creeks, seas and oceans, which were avoided by other ethnic nationalities. It is ironic however, that these areas, hitherto considered inhospitable and unproductive have proved to be the honey pot of the Nation called Nigeria. The environment of the delta is a vibrant one, endowed with amazing natural resources top of which is crude oil, discovered in 1957, long after the death of Tuburu. The crude oil extracted on and offshore, has sustained and continues to sustain the Nation since independence in 1960.

A glaring feature of the Niger Delta is the mixture of forests and waters. For example, one can find freshwater swamps which are usually dominated by raffia palms and timber as well as tidal waters/rivers zone that is characterized by mangrove forests. The area is also blessed with tropical rainforest which is identified by a predominance of short herbaceous plants, shrubs, very tall canopy capped trees, as well as other trees, including commercially viable timber.

Aquatic life was the joy of inhabitants of the delta in days gone by. They were content with life and did not need to move far a-field for their basic requirements. In addition to various descriptions of fish, crabs, shrimps and shellfish, wild life was also in abundance. Hunters never lacked hefty game as animals dashed desperately from beat to beat, on citing these unfriendly elements, called humans. The above idyllic scenario was however overturned by the insidious intrusion of 'civilization' or 'modernism.' This inevitably gave rise to the wholesale ravishing of the land, seas and oceans in the name of crude oil exploration and exploitation. This turn of events has led to the near extinction of rare and exotic animals as well as aquatic mammals and fish. As unbelievable as it may sound, inhabitants of the Niger Delta survive on imported fish! "How can a people whose occupation is fishing, be dependent on imported fish?" may be the natural reaction of the cynic but that does not remove the reality. The environment has been severely irreparably degraded.

IN THE BEGINNING

There are two areas of agreement among historians concerning the Izon (Ijaw) nationality. The first is that the name of their progenitor is Ujo and the second, that they are usually the original and indigenous inhabitants of wherever they are found and speak a language that's distinct. Professor J. S. Coleman who is regarded as one of the founding fathers of African studies in the U.S.A stated the following about Ijaws in his book, 'Nigeria: Background to Nationalism.' "...As perhaps the most ancient in West Africa, whose language has little or no affinity with any other in Nigeria."

The same sentiments were expressed by G. T. Stride and C. Ifeka in their book, 'Peoples and Empires of West Africa 1000-1800' when they said, "Some of the oldest inhabitants of the Atlantic Coast are the Jola, Pepoh and Sorer of the Sene-Gambia and the Ijaw of the Niger Delta must be included among the most ancient of the coastal settlers."

Dr. P. A. Talbot, acting Resident of Benin Division in 1920, agreed with the above assertions. He said, "This strange people, a survivor from the dim, dim past beyond the dawn of history whose language and custom are distinct from those of their neighbours. Their (Ijaws) origin is wrapped in mystery. The people inhabit practically the whole coastal area, some 250 miles in length stretching between the Ibibio and Yoruba. The Niger Delta is therefore occupied by these strange people."

Although no one can be definite about the actual place they originated from, some speculate that South Africa was the place. Others think it was East Africa or ancient Benin kingdom. There are others who insist that it was Ile Ife in South West Nigeria based purely on folklore which bear marked similarity to those emanating from the Ife area. They also claim that the Benin connection is linked to Ife, the original birth place of the Binis? This explains why according to this school of thought, stories in Ijaw folklore always identified ADO, which could be a corruption of the word EDO as the starting point or to put it more correctly, the prelude. This category of historians hold fast to their claims and nothing can change their opinion. Then comes another exciting point of view. The Bible connection! A lot of people are not at all impressed with this idea and just shrug it off as a fancy fairy tale. It is an accepted fact that history is dynamic and definitely not static, just like emigrations and migrations, which have gone on unhindered from the beginning of time. Could historical dynamism then be the reason for the disparities?

The promoters of the Biblical angle are many. However, one of them Mr. Stephen Ekeremor claimed that he had written to the director in charge of Bible studies at Tel Aviv University, to share some interesting 'facts.' Mr. Ekeremor and others who hold this school of thought believe that the Izons in all their derivations (Ijaws, Ijons, Ezons), can trace their ancestry all the way to old Palestine and specifically, to one of the lost tribes of Israel, IJON. Please see the two maps of Israel showing the position of Ijon at the extreme North of the ten-tribe kingdom of Israel above the cities of Dan and Abel-beth-macaah. According to Biblical accounts, the Ijons were (and are) a people in Israel whose city was attacked and destroyed by the armed forces of the then world power Syria and the Assyrians. The same report also states that the invading

Assyrians eventually sent the Ijons on exile. What is not known though is whether they ever returned to their homeland or they just remained in the different parts of the world to which they were exiled.

It may be pertinent at this juncture, to draw attention to some fascinating laws observed by the Izons of old and in some instances, even today. It is informative that these same practices are found in the Bible as well. For example;

a. Soldiers are sanctified before being allowed to go on a campaign in times of war. They are first required to confess their sins before the purification and sanctification (1 Samuel 21:1-6, Leviticus 15:16-18).

b. Soldiers are forbidden from being intimate with women during campaign and while in camp.

c. Soldiers are forbidden from raping or killing women and babies except such women pose a clear and present danger (Deuteronomy 21:10-13).

d. Soldiers are strictly forbidden from taking the spoils of war. The penalty for this offence is death through mysterious circumstances.

e. Soldiers are forbidden from taking advantage of their power to rob, intimidate and molest innocent citizens. Death by mysterious means is the penalty for such behavior.

f. No woman is allowed in the camp for sexual relations, to ensure that religious and physical cleanliness is maintained. (Leviticus 15:16, 1 Samuel 21:5, 2 Samuel 11:6-11).

g. Continuous cleansing is required in camp since soldiers were sanctified for warfare (Deuteronomy 20:8, Judges 7:3).

There are other laws or regulations that are worthy of mention because of the striking similarities. These relate to diet and sanitation and are as follows;

a. All persons are forbidden from drinking or eating blood substances (Genesis 9:4, Leviticus 7,26:12-17, Deuteronomy 12:23-25).

b. Certain birds such as Eagle, Vulture, Owl are forbidden as food (Deuteronomy 14:12-19, Leviticus 11:13-20).

c. Reptiles such as python, snail, monitor, are forbidden as food except, in certain communities were they are accommodated for religious purposes.

d. A woman becomes unclean immediately after childbirth and remains so for thirty days, after which she is sanctified and made whole or pure again.

e. A woman becomes unclean during her period of menstruation and whatever she touches becomes unclean also. She is however made clean after purification. It was quite common to see mothers hurdling at verandas in days of old.

f. Touching a corpse makes a person unclean but mere washing of the hands was enough to restore cleanliness, after which the person was free to re-enter a home or village.

There are still other aspects of life, governed by age-old laws that deserve mention because of their affinity with Mosaic Law. In Ex.22:22-24 and Deuteronomy 21:19, 24, 17-21, the care of widows and orphans is advocated. The same holds true of the Izon tradition which even permits a brother to re-marry his late brother's wife and a son, his late father's wife in order to provide a secure home for the children and the woman in her old age.

Polygamy finds acceptance among the people just as marriage of a seduced girl was compulsory, unless the parents refused. Marriage with a captured woman was allowed while intercourse with animals, that abhorrent practice of sodomy and bestiality was highly prohibited. Another forbidden territory for an Izon man was marriage to his mother, sister, daughter, step-daughter and mother-in-law. An Izon woman was also not allowed to marry in the above manner. The unwholesome desire for the possessions of another was seriously discouraged in Izon land just as stealing and similar vices drew the anger of humans and gods.

It was obligatory to treat strangers well even as adultery carried severe penalties. In the event of the death of the head of the family, the first son was given the greatest share of the deceased's property.

The institution of the priesthood is another important area to note. In the days of old, every Izon community had priests and a chief priest and priestess who had the primary responsibility of mediating between the gods and the citizenry. Supplications to the supreme deity (*Temearau, Woyingi, Tamuno*), usually preceded the mediations. The role of the priesthood being all encompassing took care of all spheres of life and no aspect was exempt from its influence or intervention. In times of war, it is the chief priest or priestess who usually determined the persons to be allowed to join the regiments. They also determined the number and ensure that the soldiers were adequately sanctificated. All this was done after due consultation with the all-knowing god of war, who directs appropriate course of action. The method of consultation was usually but not limited to the use of a ladder, carried by two or three men, while the priest asked questions for a direct 'Yes' or 'No' answer. Such questions would be, "Shall we go to war?" "Shall we win?" "How many men should we use?" and similar issues. This is exactly similar to the use by ancient Israelite chief priests of Urim and Thummin, for direct 'Yes' or 'No' answers.

ETHNICITY

Tuburu was born into one of the most interesting, enigmatic and dialectically diverse ethnic groups in present day Nigeria known as IZON (Ijaw), which is also the fourth largest ethnic nationality in the country. The word Izon, in all its derivations means TRUTH and this is characteristic of these simple, dignified and peace-loving people.

The Ijaws have always been an important ethnic group in this part of the world and this fact is highlighted by Major Arthur Glyn Leonard's description of them in 1906 as "---the most important tribe in the lower delta and indeed after the Ibo, in the whole of Southern Nigeria." They lived and still live in the Niger delta region of Nigeria which is believed to be the third largest wetland in the world. This area some optimist believe, still harbor great potential in spite of all it has offered the Nation. The ethnic nationality too is yet to come into its own despite its size, population and contributions to national development in terms of human and material resources. The Ijaws are currently balkanized into six States of this Country (Nigeria) for the purpose of weakening them? It is not surprising therefore, that they are minorities in a majority of the States were they are found. Little wonder then that they have continued to cry about being marginalized!

DIALECTS

The Ijaws speak many dialects. The following are some of them; *Tobu, Kolokuma, Mein, Tamo, Ibani, Nembe, Okrika, Kabo, kalabari*, etc. In modern times, this dialectic diversity has found unity in the umbrella organization called, Ijaw National Congress {INC}. There is also a dynamic youth wing, known as Ijaw Youth Council (IYC). Even before the emergence of the INC and IYC, the people knew and identified with each other through cultural and clan activities. There was never any confusion as to who belonged where and who their brethren were. While detractors of the nationality posited that the many dialects would be a source of disunity, it is interesting to note that, that has not and is not likely to happen. The Ijaw people were and are firmly grounded in their roots. The family tree of these indomitable people is anchored securely by a very deep taproot, from whose stem blossoms myriad beautiful and bountiful branches.

CLANS

There are very many clans in Ijaw land. These are homogenous units that evolved according to lineages of brethren who dispersed to found separate towns or communities. Tuburu was born into one of the most important of these clans, known as *Tarakiri*. The following are some sister clans of *Tarakiri; Oporoma, Nembe, Mein, Opokuma, Kolokuma, Ogboin, Ogbia, Andoni, Okirika, Kalabari, Operema, Gburan, Kumbo, Seinbiri, Apoi, Tuomo, Ogbe-Ijo, Akassa, Biseni, Okodia, Opobo, Kabo, Ibani, Tungbo, Zarama, Ekpetiama, Gbaramatu, Arogbo, Olodiama, Kumbo, Boma, Ogbein, Oyiakiri, Opokuma* and many more. The evolution of clans is a natural process of multiplication of the human race and in the case of the Ijaws, signifies the spread and increase of the virile and fertile children of UJO, who would certainly be very proud if he could see them today! Even so, his scions believe that he blesses them from the spirit world. The power and ability of human beings to organize themselves into manageable units as exhibited by ancient Ijaw people, is an interesting process that appears to have been going on from the time Homo sapiens came into a realization of who they truly were. The ability of certain groups to develop written modes of communication, create intricate art forms and refined styles of managing themselves, set them apart from other less ordered entities. But by and large, all human settlements have had some form of organizational structure which differentiated them from their reptilian neighbors.

TARAKIRI CLAN

HISTORY

According to oral accounts and colonial records, the origin of *Tarakiri* is traceable to their progenitor ONDO-pronounced, *{undu.}* He lived in the area generally referred to in modern times as *Toru-Ibe* and the hinterland in the region of Benin, South-South Nigeria. At some point, neighbors who were difficult to live with appeared. In particular, It is speculated that the Oba of Benin became so oppressive that he even caused the land of Ondo to be seized and in addition, imposed heavy levies on him and his people. Being of a gentle and peaceful disposition one would presume, he decided to leave his homeland in search of a less traumatic environment. This singular action of Ondo set him apart as a man of integrity and courage, traits that were later displayed by his descendants. The move also proved that he was a man of vision and foresight who realized that the change of environment could only bring him more opportunity, prosperity, progress and above all, the peace essential to the achievement of his heart's desire. From all accounts he achieved all the above and more, founding great dynasties, which have continued to wax stronger by the day. Ondo had three sons including *Tarakirowei,* the founder of *Tarakiri* clan, *Kolokumowei* and *Opokumowei.*

MIGRATION

The migratory pattern of Ondo and his children is important from the point of view of giving a clear picture about their lifestyles, which invariably shaped the character and way of life of the entire Ijaw people. Oral and colonial accounts indicate that the first place of settlement of the founding father Ondo was a community called Aboh, on the banks of the River Niger. When his family started expanding, it must have become clear to all of them that the available land area would eventually be too small for them. With this realization came the certainty of relocation. Sooner or later they were on the move. They wandered from place to place and finally pitched camp at Amatolo, a promising little village on the banks of Sagbama Creek. The great Ondo died in this community. Realizing that the land was too confined to serve their collective interests, two of the brothers migrated eastward and settled in the neighborhood of Sabagria along the Nun River. These two founded *Kolokumo* and *Opokumo*.

Tuburu's ancestor Tarakiriowei, believed to be the oldest and most powerful of the brothers, opted to remain in Amatolo. The family's presence there is believed to be centuries ago. They were however forced to disperse as a result of a dreadful war with their in-laws, the *Mein* people.

CURRENT LOCATION

As earlier stated, Tuburu's ancestors fled their home Amatolo in the wake of a bloody war with citizens of *Mein*. This war, according to colonial history, was indirectly started by a woman as an act of vengeance. According a copy of an intelligence report on Tarakiri clan sent to the chief secretary to the Colonial Government in Lagos, on 22nd February, 1932, the murder of Maluko, the eldest son of Tarakiriowei prompted the chain of events which culminated in war between the *Meins* and *Tarakiris*.

The story of Maluko is a sad one. Even though he was wealthy and had many wives, none bore him a child. Irrespective of this childlessness which caused him much heartache, Maluko's siblings envied him because of his wealth. These siblings mostly male, concretized their envy by conspiring to kill him and thereafter, take over his wives and properties. The wicked brothers actually carried out their evil plan and proceeded to appropriate Maluko's wives and properties. However, the brothers failed to plan for the bitter reaction of Maluko's only sister Komboye. They underestimated the deep bond and love between sister and brother.

Discerning persons in the community predicted that there would be an explosion of sorts when news of her brother's death reached komboye. As it happened, it was Maluko's brothers' who inadvertently detonated the emotional bomb. They informed Komboye, who came on a visit to Amatolo from her *Mein* base that her brother died of natural causes and that he left all his wives and worldly goods to them. Komboye was not convinced by the story and carried out discreet investigations on her own. What she uncovered was terrible. Her beloved brother had been brutally murdered for no reason, other than the inordinate greed of his own lazy siblings. The brothers discovered too late that their treachery proved so costly that it caused a permanent dislocation of their entire families. Konboye, who herself was also childless was not prepared to just wail, lament and swear at the perpetrators of the dastardly act. No way! She was determined to get even and nothing was allowed to stand in her way. She felt confident that the only cause of action opened to her was to plot a decisive revenge, not only to teach the brothers a lesson but to ensure that justice was done. As an only sister, Maluko had been a constant source of encouragement for her. He always offered his broad shoulders for her to cry on, in her distress at her inability to conceive after many years' marriage.

With a heavy heart but full of determination, Konboye went back to her marital home in *Mein* clan. She told them a tall tale about how the *Tarakiris* were killing *Mein* people without provocation. She knew very well that no *Mein* man would tolerate such insult and that reprisal attacks would be carried out to redeem their image. She also predicted that in the surprise attack which the *Mein* people were sure to launch many *Tarakiris*, Maluko's killers inclusive, would be killed. That way, the death of her treasured brother Maluko would have been avenged albeit, vicariously by her.

The *Meins* did not disappoint and wasted little time before embarking on a full scale war against the *Tarakiris*, concentrating in the region of Amatolo as instructed by their informant. According to the colonial intelligence report, the war was protracted and was the primary reason the *Tarakiris* left Amatolo and dispersed in all directions. Some of the clan can now be found along the Nun River and the neighborhood of Yenagoa Creek, while others are found along the Forcados River and Bomadi Creek.

SOCIAL ORGANIZATION

The social structure in Tuburu's life time was less defined. However, there was always a cultural or religious head whose authority was respected and accepted by all. This leader was also a repository of traditional knowledge and it was common for individuals or representatives of communities to refer to him for clarification on diverse issues. The clan head was also the final arbiter in land disputes and similar matters. He also served as a unifying force by presiding at seasonal festivals and other important ceremonies which were of great significance to all Tarakiris.

The Tarakiri clan then, as now, was united under a clan head {Pere} with the title of *Kpadia*, a First Class stool. While it was not necessary in ancient times for a *Pere* to be handed a staff of office before being recognized formally, the same cannot be said about contemporary ones. It is now compulsory for a clan head to be handed a staff of office by Government, usually symbolized by the Governor of a State where the clan is. This is the only way by which a traditional ruler's stool can be validated. The implication of this development is a source of worry for advocates of an independent traditional institution which is seen as the true custodian of a people's culture, tradition and value system. The *Pere* holds office for life but with this Government recognition business, he can be 'de-stooled' or dethroned for 'bad behavior' by the same Government at any time. He usually operates or functions with chiefs representing various branches of the clan who together make up the clan's Council of Chiefs.

At the community level, there are usually elected town heads known as *Amananaowei,* as well as elected town governments or Community Development Committees- CDCs, a youth body and a women's wing, all with varying tenures. These organs function according to the constitutions drawn up by their people. In some communities, the *Amananaowei* holds office for life while others prefer tenured holding for one, two or more years as the case may be.

TRADITIONAL RELIGION

Traditional African religion dominated the belief system during Tuburu's era. The mediative role of lesser gods as well as the overriding supremacy of a great God {*Temarau, Woyingi, Ayiba, Woyin, Oyin*, etc) was taken for granted. Since the people lived so close to nature, they were intensely affected by the earthy environment surrounding them. Little understood occurrences or phenomena were routinely ascribed to that impersonal friend and foe, called *Oru*(god). The priest or priestess, as representatives of the gods attracted reverence from the adherents of traditional religion. Almost all inhabitants believed in the powers of the various deities who were ever ready and seen to impose severe sanctions on erring members of the public. It must be stated that traditional religion is still very much a part of our culture today though practiced with less ferocity, primarily because of western influence and of course, Christianity. It is interesting to note that many Christians have found it difficult to make a draw a clear line between their Christian beliefs and the traditional religious belief systems. The push and pull of the two continue to affect their lives.

ECONOMIC ORGANIZATION

The Izons were and still are predominantly fisher folks, relying on seasonal pond bailing, netting and trapping. However, they also farmed and still farm at subsistence level. They have always traded with their immediate neighbors either by barter or cash in whatever form. Certain large markets have always existed, attracting traders not just from within but also from neighboring ethnic groups, as well as merchants from Ibo land. The situation has not changed much since then, except that the markets are now more and of course larger. Markets in Agbere, Tuburu's home town, usually hold every four days and are counted as *akanbai, akanla mbai, akanbombai, biribai* and *foubai*. It was common practice in those days for about ninety per cent of traders to assemble by *akanbai,* eve of the market day and interestingly, the practice has remained with the people up to the present age. Best bargains were guaranteed on this day and retailers would take full advantage to stock up and make huge profits.

INTER AND INTRA ETHNIC RELATIONS

In ancient times, the Izons cultivated good and lasting relationships through inter and intra clan marriages and alliances as well as covenants based on war. Intra communal misunderstandings in those days were mostly but not limited to disagreements in the sharing of fishpond proceeds or the boundaries of ponds or farmlands. During the life-time of Tuburu, Agbere community had running battles with some neighbors and communities, chief of which were Ofonibengha and Ikpidiama. These battles led to loss of lives and properties and generated a lot of bad blood. In some cases, the warring communities entered into peace pacts, to forestall future attacks. One such pact was between Agbere and Ikpidiama, a small village not too far from Agbere.

In modern times though, alliances are based more on mutual economic benefits and filial sentiments. There used to be deadly inter ethnic wars in early times but misunderstandings are better managed these days through more formal judicial systems established in the country. Granted that fights still break out from time to time but more lasting conflict resolution mechanisms are now in place. The same is applicable in intra ethnic conflict situations. Feuds are not nursed forever or from generation to generation unattended. They are getting resolved through the intervention of the various Councils of Chiefs or similar bodies.

AGBERE; TUBURU'S BIRTH PLACE

HISTORY

Oral history has it that Agbere community was first established on the banks of the Forcados River, opposite a town known as Kpakiama in present day Delta State. Their founding father Agbereowei, was said to have migrated to this site as a result of internal strife and wars waged by neighbors in his former home. Even as Agbereowei was relocating, so were his brothers Sampou, Angalabiriowei, Ebedebiriowei and Ogelle, who settled not too far from each other. The two communities of Agbere and Kpakiama lived peacefully for many years before a serious dispute erupted. It is believed that trouble started when the wife of the strongest man *olotu-owei*, of Kpakiama betrayed him. She took an Agbere man as her lover. The *olotu-owei* was subsequently beheaded by his enemies ostensibly, spearheaded by the love-struck Agbere man. Everyone in the affected communities suspected that the *olotu's* wife was responsible for the murder of her husband. Inevitably, there was palpable tension in both communities because of accusations and counter-accusations.

Many feared that full-scale war would break out between these hitherto friendly neighbors. The Kpakiama people were so infuriated by the unwarranted beheading of their *olotu-wei* due to the treachery of the man's own wife that they vowed to avenge his death. Following tradition, they consulted the oracle to determine who the real culprit was. The gods answered and they were satisfied. Their consultations revealed that Agbere had more to gain than lose by the *olotu's* death. The motive was clear. With the Kpakiama *olotu* dead, Agbere could overrun them in no time at all. There was no need to waste further time on divinations about the most auspicious time to attack. Immediacy and the element of surprise were therefore used by the Kpakiama people against their Agbere neighbors. What did they do under the circumstances? Something ingenious, strategic and simple, designed not only to frighten and immobilize but also to cause an exodus from the offending community. They caused some plantain plants to be planted upside down on Agbere soil. The Agbere people understandably viewed the action of their neighbors as a calamitous abomination! Panic gripped all the inhabitants. The soil was no longer fit for human habitation and had to be vacated without delay. The sacrilege was too much for the community to bear and they had no choice than to pack up and leave that site, forever!

LOCATION

The Agbere citizens were directed by divine providence to a location a few miles below the confluence of the Nun River with the Forcados River. It is likely that the oracle's aid was sought in the choice of a harmonious settlement. The settlers were assured not only of their security but prosperity as well, at the new location. They made discrete inquiries about their new neighbors and being satisfied, decided to pitch camp there. The war weary Agbere people decided to settle permanently on the bank of the Nun River since they found the environment peaceful and fertile. They have remained there ever since. The place has been good for them and they have prospered. However, there were certain experiences that they wished escaped them, like envy and blackmail from some groups. All the same, Agbere citizens can proudly say that the Almighty has been with them over the centuries, lovingly piloting their affairs. Their cohesion in times of trouble stood them in good stead and made them strong.

This is the Agbere climate and environment where Tuburu was born. A community of proud, powerful, industrious and prosperous people. It is believed that Tuburu was born at this permanent location in the mid 1800s. His birth was effortless and he was a tranquil and happy child who brought joy to his parents, said oral historians. Even at a young age, his maturity and collectedness was a source of wonder to his mother who could not help fantasizing about a great future for her strong and handsome son. Discerning elders predicted that the child's bright star would make not only him but Agbere famous some day. They also foresaw loads of trouble as well as prospects in the young child's future and predicted that he would vanquish his opponents, no matter how difficult the struggle. Witches and wizards could not be wished away as they were seen hovering in the horizon, attempting to blacken the child's star. Their efforts proved futile, as the light emanating from the young Tuburu's aura was much too powerful for the agents of destruction.

GEOGRAPHY

Agberc was and is still situated in the Niger Delta right on the bank of River Nun. It is surrounded by intermediate creeks and streams and is on the oil palm zone. The area is swampy and erosion prone, particularly during the floods. Rain falls generously from March to November and there is excessive humidity. People in this community cultivate small farms of yam, cassava, plantain, sugarcane, pepper and sweet potatoes. The wild life that was abundant in Tuburu's day is almost extinct due to oil exploration and exploitation.

EUROPEAN CONTACT AND TRADE

History has it that Agbere people first came in contact with Europeans while trading and acting as middlemen in the trading stations of Brass and Akassa in the early 19th century.

The relationship between them soon turned sour when the 'strangers' decided to extend their trading tentacles beyond acceptable boundaries. The trading companies sent steamers up the Nun River about 1860 and this action was viewed so gravely that the steamers were shot at. In return, the Europeans were so angry with the indigenes that the community was shelled by a gunboat.

Agbere people considered the actions of the intruding Europeans so humiliating that they vowed to retaliate-in their own time. That was why in 1867, seven years after the gunboat incident, another attack was carried out against the Europeans who continued to ply the waterways. They used cannons and guns acquired meanly from Awka Ibo blacksmiths for the attack which was off and on for about four months. The Europeans were incensed by the 'unwarranted' attack and resolved to teach the recalcitrant people a lesson. Four gun-boats were dispatched to bombard the town as a 'final solution.' Indeed, it appeared to be so since no other attack by either side was recorded again. However, evidence from this 'war,' comprising numerous shell cases of twelve pound shells preserved in the community have sadly been washed away by erosion.

GOVERNMENT INSTITUTIONS

It is interesting to note that possibly as a result of the 'intransigence' of Agbere people, the colonial trading company decided to establish a military post in the town in 1886. The colonial documents stated that the Chartered Royal Niger Company ran the military post for many years before eventually handing it over to the colonial government in 1900. The same records also stated that a native court was established in Agbere, in 1901 while a government school was opened in 1912 and closed in 1916. Reasons were not given for its closure, just as inhabitants and neighbors alike were getting used to the idea of the white man's method of education.

TUBURU: FUTURE WARRIOR

PARENTAGE

—————————

Tuburu's mother was Abuwerimo, daughter of Ogorika of Trofani and Eiye, of Tambiri quarters Agbere, all in present day Bayelsa State, South-South Nigeria.

He was named **TUBURUBUODE**, which means they have moved northward. This implies that a movement took place in the community possibly at the time of his birth, thereby confirming his birth place as the permanent and present location of Agbere. Chroniclers of village history attest that the families of his parents were well known and had no recent history of insanity or leprosy, two dangerous ailments dreaded by all reasonable people. Both families were also recognized as highly fertile, with strong and handsome ancestors of note. In fact, some of the greatest warriors in the history of Izon-ebe were traced to Tuburu's paternal lineage. With this rich background on both sides, it was expected that a lot of good would come out of the union between Abuwerimo and Eiye. There was no doubt in any one's mind that the children of these two would be strong, brave and prosperous, all things being equal. Tuburu's parents were simple and hardworking. Like most of their contemporaries they farmed the land, fished in the lakes and streams and hunted for their animal protein needs.

SIBLINGS

Tuburu had many siblings, twelve in all. Eight of these were half brothers and sisters. Tuburu was the second child of his mother and fourth of his father. Of all the twelve children of Eiye, only two were female and they all in turn had many children, thereby ensuring a large extended family. According to oral history, the siblings lived in harmony and loved each other very much. We can also speculate that when Tuburu became popular, his siblings were inordinately proud of him and a bit fearful for his safety. Even though Tuburu turned out to be the most outstanding of the family, it is on record that most of his siblings were men and women of worth.

CHILDHOOD

From all accounts, Tuburu had a normal and happy childhood. He was surrounded by a lively and boisterous immediate and extended family. It is very likely that he was inquisitive, vivacious and played rough with fellow kids. We can be fairly certain that he showed superior prowess in the little childhood fights that naturally occurred and sent many a playmate home in tears. He also undoubtedly showed a natural love for swimming since he lived in an aquatic environment. Excelling in all childhood games without special effort would also be taken for granted in Tuburu's early years since he was known to be bold and brash.

ADOLESCENCE

Tuburu, from all accounts was a very active youth. He was said to have been very tall and handsome indeed, imposing. His natural strength and physique attracted admiration as well as resentment from less endowed persons. It is very likely that he sat at the feet of his elders, learning the ancient arts of conversation, herbal healing, spiritual science and warfare. Like the wise men he sought to emulate, he lived close to nature, respected her laws and was well rewarded by being initiated into the secrets of the ages. Since he took part in all village activities, he must have had a string of admirers mostly women, who hung around his homestead. This logically led to his being 'given' many women to marry by parents who admired him. Whether or not he took full advantage of this is another matter which we will leave to the man himself to tell us, much later.

Tuburu's last child, Tupele lived here

THE REGENERATION STORY

Legend has it that the spirits themselves prepared Tuburu for his mission on earth. He was taken to a mythical place called EREAMA. Ereama was occupied by women only and they were the ones who fortified Tuburu and taught him the immutable laws of the universe. According to oral accounts, he was made to undergo several purification ceremonies or rituals. These were naturally veiled in secrecy and he was only released to the world after attaining newness of mind, body and soul. Ordinary people were logically not privy to all that happened, except the learned elders, who ensured that only those deserving of the honour of this age-old secret got the opportunity. Tuburu predictably became a super man knowledgeable and responsible enough about the laws of the universe not to misuse his powers. His awesome physical strength and power remained dormant more or less and he was little reckoned with. This position of virtual anonymity was to vanish almost overnight by a dramatically turn of events. The community was not only forced to take notice but became proud and at the same time, afraid of the young Tuburu. How this ambivalence shaped future events in the life of Agbere and that of the young man makes for an interesting study in human behaviour. This aspect of his life can be compared to the lives of similar persons in history whose greatness was often not recognized until some momentous occurrence exposed them to public glare. From that point on, their lives were no longer their own as the mission for which they were released to earth, gets under way in earnest. Tuburu's case was not different. He remained a fixture in the consciousness of the people of the Niger Delta until his unexpected and controversial transition.

STRIFES AND WARS

A GIANT EMERGES

An exciting incident brought the young Tuburu, to the notice and attention of the whole community and beyond. Citizens of Agbere still recount the story with pride. There is however, a minor point of disagreement as to the actual period the incident took place, which takes nothing away from the import of the event. Was it before or after his regeneration or rebirth? This was and is the big question. All agree that an expedition took place but the issue that has continued to provoke lively debate still remains. At what period in his life was the expedition organized?

This little 'confusion' notwithstanding, it is widely accepted that Tuburu would have been about twenty years old at the time the community decided to inspect some fishponds being encroached on by their neighbors, the Abuerto people. The elders agreed that only proven and battle tested men would be chosen to make the trip. The reason for this stringent qualification was simple. Those were volatile times and it did not take much to start a fight that could snowball to full blown battle so great care had to be employed in the selection of expedition teams. While the identification process was going on, Tuburu caused a stir and indeed amusement by begging to be included. The people laughed and told him to forget it because he was too young and inexperienced to be included in such a delicate journey. This was a mission for crack fighters only. Amateurs were definitely out they insisted. He pleaded passionately and finally, one Slaboh from Kakarabiri quarters told the selectors to allow the young man join the team since he appeared to fully understand the implications of the expedition.

On the appointed day, the party got to the location and discovered that unauthorized persons from the neighboring community were actually digging ponds on their land. Predictably, a fight ensued as accusations and counter accusations reverberated. As happens in situations of heightened tension, a man from the offending community attacked the Agbere team and was killed. All the members of Tuburu's team got frightened and agitated. They fully realized that there could be an escalation of hostilities when news of the death reached the other community. The implications were indeed grave and the group virtually abandoned their assignment. They forgot that there were traditional rites to be performed under the prevailing laws to show proof of the demise of the enemy. In all this confusion, one man alone remained calm and collected, Tuburu. He quickly volunteered to undertake the task of preparing the body of the deceased in the traditional manner. A task he undertook courageously, leaving no one in doubt about his abilities and leadership qualities. By this singular action, Tuburu demonstrated his extraordinary powers for the first time and was thus hailed by all when news of his amazing feat reached the village. The incident also marked the beginning of his recognition as olotu or hero of Agbere. You can be sure that he was never denied another opportunity to prove his mettle or to defend the community again.

Traditional Collection of Arsenals of War used by Tuburu

(1) *Okponu or Spear*

(2) *Agbodor or Sword*

(3) *Ogidi or Cutlasss*

(4) Ederigide

(5) A headband tied round the head with native medicine

(6) Other medicines in the basket which cannot be described

(7) Afere or plate

FIGHTING KING OF THE RIVERS AND CREEKS

Ancient Izon (Ijaw) war canoe

All accounts about Tuburu's life confirm that he was involved in some spectacular battles and wars. In all instances according to the narrators, he went into battle to redeem the image of his family or town and never for selfish reasons. His fighting arsenal was as amazing as the man himself. It consisted of a small basket containing mainly his AGBUDOU and EDERIGIDE, while his war vessel was a little dugout canoe capable of carrying no more than four persons. The basket, now made fragile by age still hangs today from the beam of his rebuilt mud house. During his fighting days, Tuburu practiced an interesting routine. Two to three days before any battle, he would consult a famous oracle at a place called *Ziboamoni Pelei,* in Agbere. As soon as an affirmative response was given, he would seek out any of his wives known to be 'clean.' This was a euphemism for not experiencing menstrual flow at that particular time. He would then embrace her passionately before confidently going into battle. As long as he remained faithful to the above ritual, victory was assured. It was also his policy to fight unhindered by companions or assistants so, he paddled his own canoe. There were only one or two instances of noncompliance with this rule when, due to pleadings from concerned members of his household, Dikagwu his son and nephew Amatolo, were allowed to accompany him.

Of all the wars Tuburu fought, non-induced as much fear in his hometown, as the ones with the traders and arms manufacturers from Ibo land. Prominent in this category were Awka merchants from South Eastern Nigeria, known in those days to be the main manufacturers of Dane guns, gun powder, gun caps and bullets. They were also renowned for their esoteric technologies, which gave them the ability to conveniently turn to any deadly wild beast like buffalo, tiger, crocodile and python and devour their enemies with relish! Any wonder then that Tuburu's kinsmen were furious with him for fighting and even killing such people, as happened on one occasion? Tuburu was so furious and disgusted with the cowardice of his people that he left for his grandmother's village Amatolo, after fortifying the community against attacks by wild beasts. He assured them that no wild animal would ever have the power to kill an Agbere person and even if any strayed into the town, it would be disoriented and eventually killed by hunters. ensured the safety of the community by single handedly mounting successful defenses from intruders of any description. It will interest you to note that the fortification subsists till today, over one hundred years after his death, according to elders and inhabitants of the town.

He really was far ahead of his peers in wisdom and knowledge and must have been bitterly frustrated by the timidity and 'blindness' of the townsfolk. All the activities he carried out in defense of friends, family and community combined to spread his fame far and wide. His incredible ability to annihilate opponents, seemingly effortlessly was the talk of the entire Izon- ebe and beyond.

As a result of this, he was called by several sobriquets such as, *Ogbajineke-* meaning disperser of the market. Tales abounded about how the mere mention of his name or indication that he was around, caused all traders to pack up their wares for the day and disperse in all directions! Some others were, *Odudu*= the feared one or the terror. *Angulubiangulubia=* the dreaded or fearsome looking one. *Keme-ankonukonukedi=the* one who's always looking at another's neck-sizing up the opponent's neck. *Awei-kpo-kile-kpo* = discretion is the better part of valor.

Tuburu also played an active part in the war between Agbere and Ikpidiama that eventually led to a peace covenant or pact among the two communities. The strangeness of this covenant deserves brief mention. Tradition dictated that a stranger and not an indigene be used for the ritual if efficacy was to be guaranteed. Both communities jointly identified a man from a distant land who was found suitable for the desired sacrifice. The sacrificial process involved the unification of man and beast in a common pit. The selected stranger called Azamlala was put into a huge pit with several live domestic animals and buried up to his neck, for seven days. Legend has it that no human being was allowed to approach the site of the covenant, a beautiful sandbank during the stipulated seven days of cleansing. According to this same legend a continuous song, possibly a dirge, was heard from the area of sacrifice and only stopped after seven days and seven nights corresponding to the time of Azamlala's death. As gruesome as this incident appears to the modern person, it was an accepted and widely practiced form of sacrifice for peace, in the days of Tuburu.

NOW WE HEAR
FROM THE MAN

FAMILY MAN

It would be appropriate at this juncture dear readers, to allow Tuburu speak for himself. Everything you have heard about him up to this point has been said by other people. The man was very much alive at the time, so let's give him the opportunity to give us a detailed account of events.

I consider it a privilege to tell the world to my story. However, before I get into my adult life, it will be pertinent to highlight some aspects of my youth that only I can effectively recount.

Not much is known about the true nature of the so-called regeneration event which actually took place in my youth. There have been many misrepresentations over the years, with some uninformed individuals ascribing my powers to demonic alliances. I can tell you categorically that nothing can be farther from the truth. I was a very curious and bright young man who was never satisfied with, *"ey*, you are too young to understand such things! *Apoo*, stop asking foolish questions and go play with your mates, *muzoru!"*

This attitude of my elders only increased and fueled a greater sense of inquisitiveness in me. I always pleaded respectfully to be instructed. No matter how hard they scolded, I remained resolute and in time, they relented and started including me in their conversations. This was the real beginning of my initiation into the mysteries of the universe. It was not easy to earn the trust of the wise old men but once they took me under their wings, there was no looking back. They knew that the sacred secrets were safe with me, my youth notwithstanding.

Do not misunderstand me. I did not become a recluse or abandon my normal pursuits, at least not in the beginning. I hunted with determination and brought home plenty of choice bush meat. I also fished and farmed to ensure that we lacked nothing in the family. My favorite pastime was swimming. My brothers Asima and Bogha could never resist a dare from me, even though I always managed to beat them, swimming across our river in twenty strokes flat, then basking in the sun while waiting for them to come ashore! On some occasions I would quickly start a fire and throw in some fish to roast, for good measure! Or just do several dance steps in the wide endless stretch of sand. Folks, I can assure you that my *Pinge* was simply phenomenal, believe me. Oh, how carefree our days were when troublesome inhabitants of some good-for-nothing villages did not attack our kit and kin or encroach on our farmlands or fishponds to annoy us!

I can still see the monkeys and gorillas jumping from tree to tree with their baleful eyes, as well as the indescribably beautiful birds flirting with each other. The dense jungle was alive with all kinds of creatures, while the river teemed with a great variety of fish, easy to catch without any complicated gadgets. It was quite simple to catch fish with bare hands. All one needed to do was stand in the water, ankle deep, allow the fish to nimble at one's toes and just ease the hands down, then grab! Swimming back to town was usually more leisurely, as we shouted jokes back and forth in-between strokes.

Another sport I always took very seriously was wrestling. Formal wrestling matches were a big affair in Agbere in my day, with supporters of the contestants gyrating to the intense *Ogele.* The appearances of the wrestlers added to the excitement. We usually painted our bare bodies with white chalk and tied heavy bells around our waists which jingled as we danced spirited at the head of the *ogele.* Added to this was the sexy *Okpa,* which only covered the essential parts of our glistening bodies! It is on record that I was never beaten at any wrestling competition and the ladies were always beside themselves with excitement and admiration, virtually throwing themselves at me, while the men stewed in envy. Frankly who could blame them when all the beautiful girls had eyes for just one man, me! The fact that I was also tall and handsome only compounded matters for my opponents. As is natural with human cyclical development, my carefree days were over only too soon, as events forced me to concentrate on the preparation for my life's work or should I say, my calling? It would have been so easy to get carried away by the adulation and popularity I was enjoying but that would have been an inexcusable waste of my gifts and talents.

I was well prepared by my teachers over a period of many years. The training was gradual and strictly out of the public domain. It called for total commitment, dedication and strict discipline on my part, as well as unwavering loyalty and fidelity to the ideals of the masters. Contrary to popular belief, there was no worship of inanimate objects, just a systematic study and application of the laws of nature as understood by my teachers and later by me. For the sake of keeping the sanctity of the teachings, I cannot reveal much but will give just a brief overview of only the much talked about and much misunderstood regeneration or purification ceremony.

I was taken bodily to a mystery abode known as EREAMA, deep in the universe. The place was so beautiful that I lack words to describe it adequately, suffice to say that it must be the dwelling place of the

Supreme Creator of the all the universes. I was totally enveloped in a cozy aroma of love, like the embrace of all the blessed mothers of Izon-ebe. Such a vast domain must understandably be filled with countless souls but I was surprisingly aware of only my few guides. Another peculiar thing was the ease I felt. Even though this was supposed to be a strange land, there was no sense of anxiety or stress. The environment looked familiar and this was one of the many paradoxes I experienced.

My tutelage started in earnest when my teacher, ancient yet ageless appeared and proceeded to instruct me in solemn silence. How long did the studies last? I sincerely cannot tell you. It may have taken quite a while but on the other hand, it seemed like all I needed to know was imparted to me in a flash! I will not blame you for asking if such is truly possible. Not being so sure, I must conclude that the instructions took some time. At the end of the period, it was powerfully impressed on me that the sacred and immutable laws of nature must be upheld at all times. This fact was, in my opinion actually branded into my brain. So powerful was the impression that I cannot describe it any other way. You will like to know what these laws are I'm sure and if my assumption is correct, it only makes you an inquisitive human, which is as it should be.

So, what are these laws? They are no other than the time tested simple truths of harmonious living, which compel the cosmically conscious to watch their actions, words and deeds. One must be acutely aware that every behavior is monitored by our unseen higher selves. These higher selves or senses I am informed are, in every heart, mind and also in every eye and ear. How about that? In my war-like era, it meant that I dared not intimidate anyone because of my perceived powers or attack people willfully just to prove that I had extraordinary strength. The only way to ensure continued victory over one's various enemies was to engage in just and justifiable fights. This was the secret of my successes, which many termed magical or mystical or even diabolical.

Of all the experiences I had in EREAMA, one stood out. The awe inspiring DEATH to LIFE ceremony. This purification exercise was performed by a universal teacher, enveloped in a cloud of what I can only describe as brilliant but muted bluish white light. My old self was virtually 'skinned' off and a new one exposed. The wise one was assisted by numerous beings of light floating in the cloud above my head. But pray, where was my 'real' body as all this was going on? This is a question I have asked myself countless times. The reason is simple. I saw a physical body, which resembled mine standing erect in a pool of golden light, while at the same time I was also floating joyously in a balloon-like cloud with the wise one. It was absolutely spectacular and beyond me to express in words. I was still taking it all in, when a gentle, almost whispery voice brought me back to earth.

"You must now go back and practice all we have taught you with fidelity," the voice said and continued.

"Remember that nature holds everything you need. Be it for good health, prosperity, peace or harmony. Respect her in all ways and she will reciprocate lavishly. Keep sacred our teachings and impart to those who are worthy, with the highest sense of responsibility, discrimination and tact. Our love surrounds you always and we await your glorious return at the appointed time." My heart was full of thanks, inadequately expressed repeatedly thus; *Oyin mmbana, mmbana! Bena-otu mmbana! Yin-otu mmbana!*

Haven been reborn into a finer mold, it became incumbent on me to maintain the highest level of maturity and sense of responsibility at all times. The practice of equity and fairness was to be rigidly applied in all my interactions and relationships and I did my best to do this. My main occupations were fishing and farming and I owned a very big plantain farm. I usually used community labour for harvesting the plantains on a sharing formula of first harvest for me and the second harvest for my assistants, provided that the first harvest was more than the second. This method of work was acceptable to all, thereby ensuring the permanent absence of labour disputes. I also employed the same system with the fishermen when it was time to bail my fish ponds.

THE MARRIAGES

I became a more reflective person after my Ereama re-birth. Even though I was still jovial and took part in normal games, I also made out time to consciously commune with my spiritual teachers and this strengthened me greatly. It was during this period that I volunteered to be part of a dangerous expedition to inspect the communal fishponds. My patriotic activities in the forest earned me a wonderful present from the blue blooded ABORO family of Ayama quarters. The family head not only gave me the title of OLOTU but also encouraged me to marry his ravishingly beautiful daughter ETOBOERE. The young lady's mother ETOBOR was from ENWE in Isoko, in present day Delta State. I happily obliged and in a few weeks, the formalities were concluded and she became my first wife. She eventually gave me four great and dynamic children namely, Alale, Dorgu, Joe Flint and the only girl Peredewari. As my fortunes improved, I married another lady called Arisinde, a daughter of Ayaowei of Tuburukunun in Agbere who bore me five children. They are Dikagu, McIntosh, Ayaere, Okpubiri and Feikibele. As people became more and more interested in my activities, two more wives were given to me, this time from PATANI in present day Delta State. They are Berekumor, who bore me several children, though all died and Engoboriagha, with whom I had three children and I named them, Tamarabebe, George and Tiger. Before marrying my last wife, whose manner of coming into my life will be related later, allow me to briefly acknowledge two women from UMUORU and NDONI also in present day Delta State, who also bore me four children Arisima, Funtua, Agorodi and Oguta.

Now to the memorable incident, that brought me my last wife. I was going on a visit to some relatives and the route took me past Amassoma a fairly large town. Traveling dignitaries were expected to pay courtesy calls on important chiefs along the route and I was no exception. It was in fulfillment of this obligation, as well as a desire to visit members of our extended family the Goins, that I stopped over at Amassoma. The *Amananaowei* received me warmly. In a matter of minutes, news of my arrival spread through the town and before long a crowd had gathered. Some people were just curious since much had been said about me in the Niger Delta, while others wanted to touch or see me in the flesh. One particular individual carried his interest beyond the ordinary. It was the ANDAOLUTU of the town who felt offended at the attention I was getting. He boasted that there was none like him.

"Why are all these people gathering to see this man?" He fumed. "I am the real *Olotu*. Have I been felled by any man? I am the greatest wrestling champion in the land.You people are very stupid for wasting your time on this nobody that I can beat in a flash!" He boasted.

The tirade continued. He claimed that he was the greatest and the strongest in all the rivers and creeks and wanted me, out of the area. At this juncture, my conscience incited me to challenge him to prove his mettle. No self-respecting *olotu* ever allows spit to be scooped in his mouth in the front a crowd and just keeps quiet. It is not done! Such behaviour will not only bring shame to the *olotu* but to his host and the whole community from which the challenged *olotu* hails. I Tuburu, could never betray my community nor my host and I had to act to redeem my image. The *Andaolotu* duly accepted to prove himself and excitement infectious. The crowd had not bargained for such an encounter but were thrilled beyond words. Some started a song and others joined, clapping and singing.

"To have two of the most talked about fighters who were also the leading champion wrestlers alive, is a treat that only the gods can offer and no sane person would want to miss seeing them in action," commented one man to a lady standing next to him.

This man's sentiment was without a doubt in the hearts of all those present that fateful day. It was decided that we would not wrestle but engage each other in a gun duel and we were also free to use cutlass. This was perfectly fine with me and my host was asked to announce the standard rules for such fights. We were to shoot as soon the umpire gave the signal, a single gunshot.

The *Amananaowei* appealed that we go to the river since he did not want blood on his land. With Dane guns in hand, we entered our separate canoes and paddled to the middle of the river, facing opposite directions until the umpire asked us to stop and turn around. The spectators who had more than doubled by this time cheered and shouted, as the countdown began. We raced towards each other as the umpire fired his shot. By the time smoke from my opponent's gun cleared, I was already in his canoe, with my cutlass poised over his neck. As I held him down by the neck, ready to deal decisively with him, the crowd shouted for leniency. Since my desire was not to kill, I spared him. As we got back on land, the traditional ruler was so impressed that he gave me his favourite daughter's hand in marriage. He insisted that I take her home with me immediately and bear him strong and handsome children. He also reconciled Bebekala, my challenger and me and we became good friends from that day on. I was naturally grateful and humbled by the kind gesture of my host, first in giving me his daughter in marriage and the reconciliation initiative. The crowd of onlookers also acknowledged everything with a big roar of appreciation. After a sumptuous meal from my generous host, we all retired for the night. I got up early the next morning, bid my host goodbye and took my very young and beautiful bride with me as I continued my journey.

I have tried in all ways, mostly by actions, to show my children the virtue of hard work and integrity. I taught them to be patriotic and not to shy away from noble tasks like defending family and community. They were made to understand that there is more to strength than the physical and that nature is the key to our survival. A lot of people were always afraid to stand up for the truth and told lies for the sake of undeserved praise. This nasty attitude always got me worked up and angry. I warned my children to keep their distance from hypocrites and to strive against hypocrisy themselves.

Some descendants of Tuburu

THE PATRIOT AND CONQUEROR

FOR COMMUNITY

Even before I was born, the Europeans had started traversing our rivers, trading on palm oil, palm kernel and slaves. Since Agbere is on a major Nun River, it was inevitable that foreign trading boats would disturb our peace and force interaction of some sort. These European trading companies established bases in Brass and Akassa on the Bight of Bonny, from where they transacted their businesses with indigenes and non-indigenes alike. As a young man, I witnessed the steamers cruising along the Nun River with its attendant unsettling influence on the entire community. Bombardments and shellings of Agbere in 1860 and 1867 were a direct result and retaliation of the hostility expressed by concerned citizens who fired at the passing vessels on a number of occasions. I can assure you that these were bitter times for our people who could not understand why uninvited strangers from unknown parts of the world, looking like fairies, had come to subdue us with their heavy guns and compel us to accept and obey them, on our own soil! *Oyinma! Akpo-an!* How the earth must have cried out for its founders. How the revered ancestors must have hissed and sighed ceaselessly in their graves! Some priests even opined that the heavy rains we experienced when rainy season had not commenced were indeed tears from the ancestors who wanted to assure us that they understood our plight. The foreigners, in the name of their Niger Chartered Company even decided to establish a trading and military post in 1886 without our consent, naturally.

During this period, the community engaged a number of towns and villages in wars, which as you can imagine required my active participation and leadership. We dealt with Ofonibengha for kidnapping an Agbere woman. It was sheer mischief on the part of the Ofonibengha people. How they thought we would fold our arms and allow them kidnap and kill innocent women just struggling to farm the land for the sake of their children, cannot be imagined. We rose up to the occasion and the occupying European forces joined us to burn and destroy the offending community because they realized that our retaliation was just. This happened in 1886.

Ikpidiama was another town we humbled. I was the arrowhead of the offensive until the inhabitants entered into a peace pact with us. Mr. Bathurst, the British agent resident in Agbere at the time asked Ikpidiama to send a delegation of eight to plead on behalf of their people who killed an Agbere woman and child. The agent had advised the people to explain to our elders and people that the deaths occurred during fighting with another town. He hoped that this personal explanation would clear up the misunderstanding. Unfortunately, he overestimated his influence because he had little or no understanding and appreciation of our cultural and traditional dictates. All the emissaries with the exception of one were killed to avenge the deaths of the innocent mother and child, to serve as a deterrent to others. Agbere people valued the lives of their citizens no matter how young or old and this point had to be made very, very strongly. This incident took place in 1895.

TREACHERY

While I was out of town, my beloved brother Bogha, a wealthy trader, took ill and died the same day. I was informed about this devastating development as soon as I returned home. According to the *Egede Okosiowei,* a blacksmith who had unhindered access into my home gave my brother a concoction. This medicine caused his death in a matter of hours. The murderer, on realizing what had happened fled the town. My grief was so intense that I could barely control my emotions. Oo! My beloved Bogha! Full of life, health and vigour, killed like a fly in a cup of water! In keeping with our laws, the coward had to be tracked down and made to account for his deed. Everyone in the community expected me to do the right thing by ensuring that the blacksmith was punished according to prevailing traditional laws. This was the natural course of action. As I made plans to find the culprit, there were thorns of sorrow in my heart. My son Dikagu and Amatolo, son of a cousin insisted on accompanying me. They reasoned that since my anger was still raw, it was not proper for me to travel by myself. I reluctantly agreed not because I had any fear of danger but to give them a sense of worth by participating in the search for the treacherous blacksmith. It was a matter of honor that the evil-minded blacksmith or his kith and kin be made to pay for the killing of my brother. The fate of this man was sealed and there was no escape. Whether the fugitive knew this or not was another matter.

We set out very early one morning with Dikagu at the helm of the canoe. I stayed in the middle *Okoun*, while Amatolo manned the stern. The mood was understandably somber, characterized by little or no conversation. After about five hours of paddling, we reached the main River Niger. At a point between Wari-iri and Otuoko along this same Niger River, we sited the blacksmith's kith and kin. They were in a large commercial boat. We immediately launched an attack and a great battle was fought that day. With the justness of our mission, the outcome was not in doubt, as victory crowned our effort. The battle was so fierce that those in far away Elemebiri heard the sound of gunfire and sent out spies to enquire. It is on record that the enemy was totally and completely annihilated.

Peace returned to my troubled heart after this battle and we went home to Agbere, fulfilled. However, the happy welcome I was expecting turned to bitter disappointment when the community chided me for killing a dreaded and feared people such as the blacksmith's kith and kin. They reasoned that since these people were known to be expert manufacturers of arms and ammunitions, there was a likelihood of retaliation on the town. It became obvious to me that their initial encouragement and insistence that I seek out and punish the murderer of my brother was mere lip service. Did they think I was going to shake hands with the criminal? I simply could not believe my ears.

Since my people were only concerned with their petty worries, I made up mind to leave for my grandmother's town, Amatolo. I assured the Agbere people that they would never be harmed by any wild animals or other intruders because I knew the secret of all those things. It did not take too much time and effort to fortify the entire community from harm for the current and future generations. A select few were given the secret methods of purification and general guidance as well as the simple rules for perpetual efficacy of the protective systems.

Having satisfied myself that the entire town would be safe no matter what, I announced my decision to leave for my grandmother's hometown. I told the people that my decision was hinged on their show of ingratitude, exhibited by their admonitions to me which were more or less based on fear for their own safety. I was very sad that my contributions to the town, which made it a no-go area for troublemakers was just taken for granted and not rewarded by thanks. Agbere became the place to avoid if you had unholy intentions because Tuburu would surely get you. Yet, my own people were too blind and narrow minded, even envious or jealous to accord me my due. They did not trust me. But will that cause me to fight an Agbere person? NEVER! The attitude of the townspeople also enraged my kindred and pitted our quarter against the other three quarters that made up the autonomous community. A fight could have easily resulted if wisdom had not been applied and I was determined that absolutely nothing would make me fight my own town, no way! I repeatedly assured them that maximum protection would be put in place by me, not just for the present but for future generations as well. I told the elders that a circumcised woman should not bathe naked at Agbere waterside and palm kernel oil must not be prepared in front of the town but at the back. Signs of abuse or noncompliance would either be the appearance of a crocodile floating patiently at the waterfront or wild animals surfacing in the town. In the event of the above happening, I gave them the remedial measures necessary for normalcy to return. Satisfied that everything had been taken care of, I traveled to Amatolo, my maternal grandmother's home with almost all members of my household.

MAN OF THE ELEMENTS

After living peacefully and happily in Amatolo for several years, I yielded to the demands of Agbere people who had led several delegations to me over the years, pleading that I return home. Being a committed patriot, I eventually agreed. There was jubilation by all well-meaning citizens when I arrived. It gladdened me immensely to note that Agbere now faced very few threats or attacks from any group. But for the killing of the Agbere woman and child referred to in another chapter, it would not have been necessary for me to fight anybody again, at least for a long time. I was happy though that our retaliation against Ikpidiama people led to a permanent truce by way of a serious *avour* or peace treaty. There was debate among the decision makers about the type of *avou*r we should accept. Everyone knew about the type we used in *Ere-ake-tei* cases, where a slave had to be produced and buried up to his neck. Thereafter, kola nuts and cassava dipped in water were placed in his mouth. Even though the slave was left to die, the two communities took an oath not to harm each other ever again. This was the accepted practice but was it suitable in the matter between Agbere and Ikpidiama people? This was the big question we wrestled with. Finally, we agreed that a slight departure from the norm would suffice. Someone then brought a slave with the interesting name of Azamlala for the *avour*. Ikpidiama and Agbere indigenes became unbroken allies thereafter, bringing lasting peace to the area. So the last battle I fought before going to hospital for a minor operation was the Ikpidiama/Agbere war.

It is worthy of note that shortly after my return from Amatolo, the community capped their gratitude by giving me several acres of land to the east of the town. Speculations that the reason for the gift was to ensure full protection of the Eastern flank of the town did not dampen by happiness at the gesture. To tell you the truth, acquisition of land was far from my mind at that time. I certainly was not the acquisitive type otherwise I would have taken as much land as I wanted without fear of challenge from anybody.

You must have noticed that I talked briefly about going to a hospital established by the Europeans for a minor operation. You must also be wondering what kind of ailment I had that required as drastic an intervention as an operation. The answer is simple. In the course of fighting, I sustained some minor wounds, which meant nothing to me. It was a surprise therefore when I started experiencing a nagging pain in my abdomen, which refused to go away. Since I was quite close to my first son Alale, I told him about the pain. He suggested that I visit the white man's hospital in Asaba-ase for a thorough medical examination. I initially rejected the idea because I had never had cause to depend on another human being, much less the Europeans for treatment or cure. All that was required for healthy living was shown to me as needed. A lot of things were also revealed to me in dream form and other forms, which convinced me beyond reasonable doubt that the white man's cures were not as good as ours. I was also reluctant to listen to my son because of the clear insight I received about a possible sudden transition. Death as we imagine it does not exist in the realm of the Creator, just transition. There was a particularly graphic picture I was shown about my eventual movement from earth. This compelled me to call some members of my family to inform them that in the event of my sudden death, my body should not be buried in a permanent way. The earth covering the coffin should be loose because I would make a physical reappearance on the third day. I assured them that there was nothing to be afraid of and made them promise to abide by my instructions. Satisfied that I would not be betrayed, I consented to be taken to the hospital.

On reaching there, we were taken to the examination room. The doctor touched some parts of my body and looked at the man assisting him and whispered something. He nodded his head two times and told us that the doctor needed to inject me with a tiny needle. The assistant who looked so much like an Awka man made me uncomfortable. He said I should open my buttocks for the injection and I did so warily. As he injected, the needle simply broke on impact with my skin. The doctor looked helpless and said he could not treat me without the injection. I then promised to return in a few days. I discussed the situation with my son Alale, who convinced me that it was okay to allow myself to be injected. We went back home to Agbere, stayed a few days and returned to the hospital for the final treatment. Since I was not comfortable with the interpreter who was assisting the doctor, I wanted him removed from the operating room. I made signs to the doctor but he pretended not to understand what I was saying and worse still, my son Alale was not allowed to be with me. I got on the operating table all by myself. *Tufia*! How could I, *Odudu! Angulubiagubia! Ogbajineke! Kemeakonkonkedi! Awei-kpo-kile-kpo*! A man of few words and plenty of action, put myself at the mercy of this knife–wielding doctor, I silently raged. Next thing I knew, there was light everywhere. My blessed mother was there, so was my beloved brother Bogha and several familiar persons who had long 'died.' I looked at the table from high above the doctor's head and saw myself immobile. The doctor was shaking his head and the assistant looked pleased. Surprisingly, I felt very light, happy and free! Could this be the meaning of the messages sent to me by my teachers? Could this be the beginning of another journey—the real journey? These were just fleeting thoughts. In no time at all, I was led away in a sea of loving vibrations.

TUBURU'S LIFE AFTER LIFE

Agbere was thrown into mourning by the news of Tuburu's unexpected passing. As the news spread across the length and breath of *Izon-ebe,* there was shock, then relief among certain elements who had dreaded his presence for years. The divergent emotional reactions were perfectly normal under the circumstances. Tuburu's family was inconsolable, little forgetting that he had admonished them against crying needlessly in the event of his demise because he would surely come back to life again. When this particular 'returning to life' scenario filtered into the community, it sent shivers down the marrows of several bones and there was uneasiness everywhere. People gathered in clusters to discuss or whisper about this unprecedented claim, never before heard of in *Izon-ebe.* Important elders started analyzing the situation critically in order to take some pragmatic steps or decisions. They reasoned that if Tuburu who was the most powerful person while alive, was allowed to come back to life, it would be the biggest mistake ever. The man would be unstoppable and will be capable of annihilating whole groups of people or communities at will. They agreed that such should not be allowed to happen. All means must be marshaled to ensure that the man did not surface ever again. He must surely remain dead, they vowed. Meanwhile, at the announcement of the death of Tuburu, all hell broke loose in the forest. Animals, reptiles and insects of all description besieged the town from all directions, making frightful noises. To say that the entire community was enveloped by untold fear and horror, would be putting it mildly. In fact, some accounts say that this behavior of the creatures of the forest preceded the formal announcement by Tuburu's son first son Alale, who was with him when he passed on. Even if he was not with his father, it would have been his responsibility to inform the elders that the greatest, the *Odudu* had fallen. Fast footsteps were heard all over the town. People ran indoors with their children. The town crier asked everyone to be calm and stay indoors because the

GREAT ONE was being mourned appropriately. There was no need to be afraid since no harm would befall anybody in the town, he assured. The creatures mourned this mighty man of the creeks, rivers and seas for three days before retreating into the forest from whence they had come. This was the first and last time this type of mourning took place in living memory. As was usual in such cases, this incident later got itself woven into the bosom of myth and legend. Many in distant places debated heatedly about the possibility of monkeys, tigers, leopards, ants, flies, mosquitoes, etc ever swarming a town as a mark of respect, recognition, honor to mourn a departed warrior. They doubted that such a feat could really take place, even for such a one as the great and indomitable conqueror, Tuburu.

There were speculations about what really caused the sudden death of Tuburu at the hands of the Asaba-Ase based colonial hospital doctor. Conspiracy theorists, averred that the assistant to the doctor was actually an Awka man, who took advantage of Tuburu's illness to avenge the killings of his kinsmen, following the death of Boagha. Others swear that the remote cause was an injury the warrior sustained in the heat of battle. This particular group claimed that during a battle between Tuburu and the Awka traders, he was hit by a poisoned spear which sent him plunging into the river. He however not only succeeded in pulling out the spear, which left a nasty gash at his side but continued the fight and returned home in triumph. This wound they said, festered and resulted in the illness that sent him to the white man's hospital. A third category of 'rationalists' swore that the conqueror was conquered by a mere bilateral inguinal hernia. They also concluded that the *Ogbajineke* was overdosed with chloroform which was the anesthesia in use in the hospital at that time.

Well readers, which account is the authentic one? Indeed should we concern ourselves with a dissection of the various theories or just draw the most rational conclusion, which is, that the unbeatable king of battle, was disgracefully snuffed out by the ineptitude of a colonial doctor, who did not know how to use the correct dose of chloroform! Tuburu died in 1895, when his services were still needed by his town and indeed all of *Tarakiri Otu and Izon-ebe*.

His body was brought to Agbere by relatives and the colonial occupiers amidst pomp and pageantry. His coffin, made with the traditional material *Du-ere gbesa,* was bedecked with fine cloths and was carried by selected pallbearers who considered it a great privilege to carry the coffin of the unbowed warrior. As was customary, a proper wake preceded his interment. Men of comparable experience performed the prescribed rituals for the departed as canon and gunshots rang out. These men gave a creditable account of themselves to the delight, admiration and awe of the massive crowd from within and outside Tarakiri. The temperature was around one hundred degrees Fahrenheit, a fitting day for a grand farewell to a deserving son of the elements. At last, it was time to commit the warrior's body to earth, opposite the town, in the *Dowei-bou.* While the immediate family had stopped crying because of their father's promise of coming back to life, the elders and leaders had a different plan of a permanent nature. People jostled and pushed for a final look, as the coffin was carried to the canoe designed to convey the body to the burial ground. The family also watched with heavy hearts occasioned by uncertainty. Could the unthinkable happen? Will the unimaginable manifest? Were the leaders trustworthy enough to honour Tuburu's last wish and not cover the grave permanently, they asked each other quietly. This uneasy speculation made crying impossible. Several people sobbed brokenly as the burial canoe, accompanied by two other canoes headed for the burial ground. The men paddled briskly in unison as all watched, unwilling to leave the waterfront until the boats crossed the river and the pallbearers carried the coffin ashore.

There was palpable tension and muted excitement in the town as the 'three days of promise' drew near. 'Will he or will he not?' were the only subjects of conversation in Agbere and in fact, the whole Tarakiri clan. On the eve of the third day, spontaneous vigil was organized by all interested citizens which meant the whole town. The expected day arrived in a blaze of scorching sunlight. All eyes were fixed on the horizon, north of the town and zoomed in on the burial bush. Perspiration poured freely down the faces of the waiting and watching crowd but none appeared to care much about sweat, damp dresses or even blistering heat. The main thoroughfare was as crowded as a dance hall, full of individuals of all ages. Some people elected to stay right at the water's edge, with ears peeled in anticipation. Then suddenly, there was a hush. Everywhere was quiet as all strained to hear a sound, a definite sound emanating from the direction of the burial bush. The sound was unmistakable. It was blood curdling and was coming from the throat of a human being. A few who were eager to witness the miracle actually fled in terror! They imagined that some ghost would bestride their land and do them in. The ambivalent feelings of fascination and fear were understandable, since no one had ever heard about this phenomenon of a dead Izon man coming back to life! They had the right to be amazed and perplexed. As the sound faded, a few brave men jumped into a canoe and off they went, for an on-the-spot assessment. After what seemed like eternity, the fact finders returned without the great warrior. Questions were thrown at them from everybody at once.

"Did you see him? How did he look? Why did you leave him behind? Was he really alive? Did you people touch him? What actually happened in that bush?" On and on the bombardment went. Much later, after giving a report of their findings to the elders, the general public's curiosity was satisfied when the people were informed that the *Duere gbesa* actually split into two when they opened the coffin and the *Odudu* was found in a crouching position! With trembling hands, they rearranged him and quickly left the *dowei bou*. Needless to say, everyone who heard the report was dumbfounded and speechless. Mixed emotions trailed this news. While family members and admirers of Tuburu expressed bitterness at this massive conspiracy, others voiced relief. The controversy raged for decades. Over a hundred years after his transition, the Tuburu saga is still generating interest and lively discussions wherever it is mentioned. Was he a villain or a man of valour, a terror or a treasure? You be the judge.

THE LEGACY AND THE LEGEND

Tuburu is remembered today as one of the greatest warriors of the Ijaw ethnic nationality, comparable to Chaka the Zulu of South Africa. His descendants are inordinately proud of him and he would also be very proud of them if he were around today. One of his grandsons became the first western educated interpreter in Izon land. Another rose to become the first African Chief Clerk in Makurdi, Northern Nigeria. While another was the physically strongest man in his State for a long time and was prohibited from fighting. Still another grandson became the first medical Doctor and Specialist in the old Western Izon Division. Another grandson became a junior Minister in the first Republic. At the level of the great grand children can be found first class Engineers, Broadcasters, Journalists and other high caliber professionals. He continues to be of service to Agbere community and indeed Izon Nationality through his grand, great and great, great grandchildren. His fame spread widely in all riverine communities, from Umoru up North to Amatolo in the South and he left his mark in one form or another along the length and breath of *Izon-ebe.*

Many have asked whether his powers were strictly physical or mainly spiritual or metaphysical. People have also wondered about the possibility of his abuse of these powers. From available information, one can posit that he was a master of the natural arts. He clearly combined his immense natural strength with spiritual and metaphysical knowledge. He was never known to overtly perform sacrifices or indulge in cumbersome rituals. The simplicity of his fighting implements, attest to his closeness and unity with nature. He was not known to forbid hordes of things like the typical animists or diehard traditional religionists. Consciousness of retributive justice informed his life style so he could not have abused either his physical or spiritual powers. The consequences of abuse were ingrained in him and his high sense of responsibility would never have encouraged such foolishness. The Creator has a way of preserving his creatures be they animals, plants or humans and the wise old people in our communities found these secrets long ago. Everything needed for the survival of the human race is given to the listeners and humble learners of every age, so Tuburu's access to this knowledge was not novel. Human beings are privileged to be given this opportunity, which they can reverently utilize and thereby live in complete harmony with their world. Contemporary society is replete with individuals living quietly and joyously with the benevolent fruits of nature, just as the ancients did. All human beings are essentially given the freedom to choose a path. A consciousness or lack of it cannot be blamed on anyone but ignorance. It is possible that certain persons called Tuburu names and ascribed his fighting prowess to demonic influences because they were too complacent to search diligently and tap from his source of wisdom and knowledge. Tuburu may have been born a star but he worked hard to make it shine brightly. There are millions who are born stars but remain dim for lack of activation or vivification.

Tuburu evoked mixed reactions from people wherever he went and this was perfectly fine with him. He could not prevent people from either admiring his impressive and handsome features or accepting his leadership, which was earned. He could also not stop people from fearing him because of his awesome feats. He was reputed to be a fair and gentle person who spoke sparingly, as all introspective and deeply cosmically aware individuals are. One of his titles *"Awei-Kpo-Kile-Kpo,"* which means 'discretion is the better part of valour' speaks volumes about the humility and commonsense of this enigmatic figure. He left empty chatter for the unserious and responded only when directly spoken to. Tuburu was basically a doer, who did not dissipate precious energy on frivolities. He was also not overly concerned with material acquisitions.

While his contemporaries were busy acquiring large parcels of land here and there, he was busy defending his community. According to the elders, Tuburu did not own a single piece of land even though he could have taken everything if he so desired. He certainly had the power to do so but chose not to. That was why he provided leadership to ward off the intrusive Europeans whose trading vessels plied the River Nun with impunity, forgetting that the territory belonged to the indigenes. The colonial intelligence reports stated that Agbere people consistently attacked their trading vessels beginning from 1860 and ended in 1867. This is no mean feat, for a so-called 'primitive' people, fighting without sophisticated weapons.

One of the most fantastic myths about Tuburu is that he owned numerous slaves whom he eliminated en-mass at some point for fear of 'pollution' of his household! In order words, he killed off all his slaves because he feared that his family was in danger of being contaminated by them. Could it be that some daring ones overstepped their boundaries and even attempted to make amorous moves in the direction of the daughters of the house? This particular story has not been substantiated and therefore falls within the realm of myth.

ETHNIC WORDS/GLOSSRY

Akanbai	-	*Market eve*
Akanbombai	-	*Another name for market day*
Akanlambai	-	*Pre-market eve*
Akpo-an	-	*This life! What a world!*
Amananaowei	-	*Head chief of a town*
Andaolotu	-	*Wrestling Champion*
Angulubiangulubia	-	*The fearsome one with dreadful looks*
Aweikpo-kile-kpo	-	*Discretion is the better part of valor*
Bena-otu	-	*Relatives*
Biribai	-	*Middle of the market week*
Dowei-bou	-	*Graveyard*
Dowei-edubu	-	*Grave*
Duere-gbese	-	*Widow's stick, special material for waving coffins*
Ebe	-	*Nationality*
Ere ake tei	-	*Forced elopement with a girl*
Foubai	-	*Market day*
Izon /Ezon-ebe	-	*Ijaw Nationality*
Keme-ankonkonkedi	-	*The one who's always looking at another's neck*
Mmbana	-	*Thank you*
Muzoru	-	*Go and play*
Odudu	-	*The feared one or the terror*

Ogbajineke	-	*Disperser of the market*
Ogele	-	*Lively dance procession*
Okoun	-	*Plank used for sitting in the dug-out canoe*
Okpa	-	*Cloth, folded to cover the loins*
Oyinma	-	*O God!Mother Creator*
Penge	-	*A fast paced dance*
Pere	-	*A King/traditional ruler of a clan*
Temarau	-	*God. Mother Creator*
Toru-abobou	-	*Mouth of the river*
Yin-otu	-	*Mothers*

BIBLIOGRAPHY

Professor J. S. Coleman: "Nigeria: Background to Nationalism," Los Angeles, 1963, Page 28

G. T. Stride and C. Ifeka: "Peoples and Empires of West Africa 1000 – 1800" 1971, Page 3

Dr. P. A. Talbot: "Tribes of the Niger Delta," 1932, Page 5

Benafari Benaebi: Ijaw Peoples Association (IPA), UK. Ijawnation@ yahoogroups archives, 7th October, 2004

Intelligence Report on The Tarakiri Clan of the Western Ijo Sub- Tribe: 22nd February, 1934

The Nigerian File Intelligence Report of the Tarakiri Clan of Western Ijo Sub-Tribe Warri Province: March 1932

Ijaw News: August 2003, Page 9

Ekeremor Stephen: "The Ijon in Israel as Recorded in the Bible," 31st May, 2001, Page 4-6

Printed in the United States
By Bookmasters